Today, Tomorrow, Hereafter

Retirement Planning and Legacy Preservation

JANET A. METZINGER, CLU, CHFC

TAKE CHARGE BOOKS

Brevard, North Carolina

Take Charge Books
PO Box 1452 Brevard, NC 28712

Library of Congress Cataloging in Publication Data
is on file with the Library of Congress.

ISBN: 978–0-9883866–7-9

Cover and interior design: Gary A. Rosenberg
Editor: Kathleen Barnes

Printed in the United States of America

To my family, the memory of my mother and father,
and my six siblings and two daughters, I love you.
And to my hundreds of clients who have meant so much
to me over 30 years as a financial planner; I hope my
clients have gained as much from our relationship
as I have from them. I thank you.

Cover image: The cover image of the apple tree is a very important one to me. The red apple represents the client, who is symbolized by the ripe fruit that we keep from falling to the ground and becoming bruised. We strive to nurture and care for the client, like we nurture and care for the apple tree—our roots solid and extending deep into the Earth and our branches offering welcome shade.

Every morning in Africa, a gazelle wakes up.
It knows it must run faster than the fastest lion or it will be killed.
Every morning a lion wakes up.
It knows it must outrun the slowest gazelle or it will starve to death.
It doesn't matter whether you are a lion or a gazelle,
when the sun comes up, you better start running.

—A FABLE QUOTED IN THOMAS FRIEDMAN'S *THE WORLD IS FLAT*

Contents

Introduction

I'm on the edge of the Baby Boom generation. I won't say which edge, but let's just say I've been around the financial planning business since the early '70s when it was an almost unheard of profession.

As the youngest of seven children, I've witnessed the aging process from a variety of viewpoints, sometimes as a bystander and sometimes actively engaged in the process with family members.

That's why I'm sharing my experience with you: to help you with the decisions that accompany the aging process, the financial bright spots and the dark ones, and perhaps to help you avoid some of the pitfalls.

I began learning my own financial lessons at an early age. At the ripe old age of 13, with my parents' approval and encouragement, I lived away from home one summer and worked as a nurses' aide in the geriatric wing of a hospital. I know it sounds strange to think of a 13-year-old on her own, but it was a different world and a safer one in those days. This sort of arrangement was not really unusual, especially for the children of large families like me.

I loved working in the hospital and experiencing life and death situations every day. I look back at one particular incident with amusement today, but it wasn't exactly funny at the time: An elderly lady had come in to the hospital and unfortunately expired shortly after her arrival. The task of wheeling the sheet-enshrouded body to the hospital's morgue fell upon a young student nurse and me. We were a little squeamish about our first trip to the land of the dead that was about to become much more "exciting." Unbeknownst to my companion and me, the lady had broken her arm before her death, so she was wearing a cast. As we wheeled the gurney through the door, we must have bumped the elbow of one of the arms laid across her chest. The arm with the cast flopped down and tagged me. I am sure my companion and I set some new land speed records that day!

Many lessons like that, and the more serious ones I learned at that tender age, have carried forward through my decades of helping people plan for their last decades of life.

My starting pay was 35 cents an hour, so I earned $14 a week. I paid $8 a week for my room and depended on hospital food, which even then was pretty dismal. But it was cheap and nourishing enough. It was unthinkable to consider a meal out or a movie.

So I went to the hospital's admin office and applied for a job on a different shift on the same floor. Since good workers were hard to find and the hospital was already familiar with my work, I borrowed an identity from a relative so I could be hired. My new job still paid only 35 cents an hour, but I had twice as many hours. I got a raise to 50 cents an hour before I left the job.

I was really on top of the world! Finally, I had a little change in my pocket and the chance to go out for a pizza and a movie once in a while.

I actually began working in the financial services industry before I even started school, when I'd monitor the radio and get commodities prices for my father, who was in the grain business. Then when I was 15, I had my first real job in the industry with a commodities broker. I am sure I was 15, because I was driving to work without a license one day and got stopped for speeding. My mother was none too pleased!

My job for the commodities broker involved taking the commodity prices off the ticker tape, standing on a ladder and continuously updating them on a huge blackboard. This was for the edification of a bunch of old fogeys who would hang out at the brokerage all day, watching the prices and making trades. I loved that job!

Later, after teaching high school chemistry, biology and physical education and a couple of years as a fifth and sixth grade teacher, I had my first job as a financial services professional.

I loved the financial services work, partly because it allowed me to be home in the evenings with my two young daughters. As a single mom, that was really important to me.

But it was also very important that, as the only breadwinner in the family, I was able to bring home enough to buy the bread. I was doing well, and soon I was to begin doing even better when my business began to branch off into retirement and estate planning. Financial planning was in its infancy in those days and only a few professionals were beginning to think of offering life-planning services, not just investment services. I was very excited to be in on the ground floor of this new profession.

In 1974, when the federal Employment Retirement Income Security Act (ERISA) went into effect, there was a whole universe of new regulations for retirement plans. From an extremely knowledgeable mentor, I was able to learn how to navigate the new regulations, which offered me more valuable lessons for the future. I had the opportunity to talk to business owners about their pension plans and the new 401(k)s.

In the late '70s and early '80s, inflation and interest rates were very high. The future picture was not very clear. Mortgage rates in the 10 percent range and high inflation rates seemed to be a permanent fixture. We never imagined a future of low interest rates and low inflation like we see today.

In those early days, I bought a house with an adjustable rate mortgage at 10.5 percent. I was lucky that rates did go down and the adjustable rate worked very well for me, unlike people in the early 2000s who got badly burned by those same adjustable rates. In those days, fixed rate mortgages were north of 12 percent.

These uncertain investment factors led many business owners to seek my help in planning for the future, so my business grew.

Monday, October 19, 1987 was one of those dates that have gone down in infamy. Black Monday was the day the stock market crashed, losing 22.61% in a single day.

It was a whole new world and not a very pretty one. People who had worked for decades suddenly found their investments had become nearly worthless. They had no idea how they would ever be able to retire.

I found myself in the perfect position to help those investors and business owners find ways to recovery from that devastating day. My existing contacts in the business community gave me the credibility to talk to companies about the retirement plans they offered and their group health insurance policies.

This book is an outgrowth of a lifetime of experience with the physical and fiscal aspects of aging. I hope I can share some of my admittedly unusual insights with my readers and clients. I know retirement can be a rocky road, and I hope some of what I've learned in nearly 40 years in the business will help you avoid some of the potholes.

—Janet Metzinger • Chartered Life Underwriter (CLU),
Chartered Financial Consultant (ChFC)
Brevard, NC • January 2014

CHAPTER 1

A New Way of Looking at the Last Third of Your Life

It has long been thought that a theorist is considered great because
his theories are true, but this is false. A theorist is considered great,
not because this theories are true, but because they are interesting.
The difference between dull and interesting is the element of surprise.
When an idea affirms unbelief, we're bored and we call it obvious.
But where an idea is counterintuitive, we're intrigued.
We then begin to ask questions.
A new theory will be noticed only when it denies an old truth,
proverb, platitude, maxim, adage or saying.
—Sociologist Murray Davis, 1971

How important is money to you?

This is the first question I ask every client.

Usually they tell me that money means security and a roof overhead for themselves and their families.

My second question: How long do you think you'll live?

If you're like most of us, you think you'll have a very long life. I plan to live to a ripe old age and I hope you do, too.

As a financial planner, I always ask my clients the third question: "What do you plan to do for the rest of your life?"

I usually get answers like, "I've always wanted to travel to China," or, "I'd love to have a cabin on a lake or a condo on the beach or an island in the Caribbean."

Part of my job is to help you make those dreams come true. The other part is to give you a reality check.

Here's just an intuitive guess: If you're reading this book, you are probably 50 or older. How do I know this? I'm not psychic and I don't have a magic spyglass. I've just seen it from my 40 years as a financial planner: Almost all of my clients first come to me when they are about 50 years old. Their children are approaching the time when they will leave the nest. College is done or nearly done.

At age 50, income and earning power are about at their peak.

This is the time when singles and couples realize they need to play catch-up, with retirement only 15 years or so away for many of them.

Very few of us expect to retire at 65 anymore and a Gallup poll shows that 37% plan to work far beyond age 65. The main reasons people work later into life today are that they really love their work and they don't want to retire or, more commonly, they realize that they can't afford to retire.

So I ask a few more questions. You can ask yourself these same questions now:

How long to do you plan to keep working?

How much money do you think you'll need every year of your retirement?

How much are you putting in your retirement accounts every year?

If you have a 401(k), IRA or other retirement account, are you paying close attention to the way your money is being invested and how much it is earning?

And here's the zinger:

How much have you saved for retirement?

And the follow up:

When did you start saving for retirement?

This is when I usually get some stumbling answers like, "Not enough, not early enough."

In this book, I'll give you some simple caveats:

1. Plan to live longer than you think you will.

2. Plan to spend more than you thought you would.

3. Plan to earn less on your investments than you thought you would.

Now this may sound hopeless, especially if you're like most of my clients, who didn't really start thinking about saving for their Golden Years until the kids were out of college.

It's not at all hopeless, but it's going to be a challenge. We'll work together to identify your goals and your personal needs, and together we'll create a plan to help you achieve your goals.

My clients fear financial stress more than they fear death. Their biggest concern is that they will outlive their money.

The dangers are that we live too long or that we die too early.

Dying too early isn't really much of a problem if you've left life insurance in place to take care of your family.

And living too long will less likely be a problem if you've made smart investment decisions.

This is the time to take a look at your lifestyle. It won't be same as when you were working, especially if you were an employee (at whatever level) with a regular paycheck. I'll go into this in much greater detail in coming chapters, but let it suffice for me to say now that receiving that last paycheck is usually an emotional blow, no matter how enthusiastically you were anticipating retirement. Change is our second greatest fear.

You've no doubt heard the adage that change is the only constant in life. It's a big part of our lives until death catches us. Aging is the most obvious and inevitable change that Mother Nature imposes upon us. But we all encounter dramatic life changes in one way or another. Children grow up and leave the nest. Marriages fail and new partners are found, or we remain single. We lose jobs and (hopefully) find new ones. Businesses succeed or fail. Serious health challenges present themselves.

When you think of the future, what does your picture look like? Clarity is not a God-given talent, so none of us can know for certain how our lives will unfold, what events will propel us on to our goals or sidetrack us. Neither can we know how we will address those events.

I like to think of the later years in life in three segments:

The Go-Go Years: From age 65 to 75 (give or take a few years)

These are the years you've earned after a lifetime of hard work and raising kids. This is the time you'll travel, perhaps enjoy a vacation home and maybe even spend winters in Florida. Of course, the lifestyle you've always wanted requires the funds to make it happen.

The Go-Slow Years: From age 75 to 85 or so

You've pretty much travelled as much as you want. You long for that rocker on the front porch and occasional visits to see the grandkids. There may be a few health challenges. You're simply not as active as you were in the early years of retirement. This is probably the time of life when your expenditures will be the lowest.

The No-Go Years: Age 85 on

These are the years when health challenges typically take their physical and fiscal toll. You may become widowed. Have you planned for this, emotionally as well as financially? Your health may deteriorate to the point where you'll need to consider relocating to a retirement home, assisted living, or even long-term care—all of which are enormously expensive. You may consider bringing help into your own home or moving in with your children. Early planning makes this less stressful on your mind and on your pocketbook.

As we make our way through this book together, along with the included worksheets, we'll also spend some time looking at the ways that expected and unexpected change affects our lives and our financial plans.

I'll also give you a few simple admonitions as we get started:

1. If you still have the opportunity, fund your retirement *before* you fund your children's college education. Yes, I know this sounds harsh, but do you think your kids are going to fund your retirement? They can get college loans. You can't get loans to finance your retirement.

2. Retirement is a three-legged stool. Social Security was never meant to fund your retirement. It is only one leg of a stool that cannot stand unless you have two-thirds of your income needs in other types of funds, including investments and personal savings.

3. Most analysts will tell you that you need 80% of your current take-home pay as you go into retirement. I think you need 100–110%. I'll tell you why.

There may be some messages in this book that are difficult to consider. We'll be talking about death, fear and finances. All of these are frequently entangled in our lives. I'm not here to sugar coat the truth, but I am also here to help you find a way to make your dreams come true.

I'm here to help you get a reality check. Maybe an island in the Caribbean is beyond any means you are ever likely to enjoy, but a cabin in the mountains might be possible. Maybe you'll need to work to age 68 or 70 to be able to save the amount you need for a comfortable retirement, but these days most of us retain our health that long or even longer.

Each person's situation is unique. I spend a great deal of time with my clients to understand what they envision, and to help them make the choices most likely to reap the results they are seeking.

Why is today's generation of workers, largely the Baby Boomers, so far behind in preparing for retirement?

Basically, they were caught between a rock and a hard place.

The rock was the traditional pension plan, which, for most of them, was the only option for retirement savings until they were at their mid-career point in about 1980 and 401(k)s began to replace pension plans. It wasn't until 1982 that 401(k) plans began to become available, then only through large employers. Federal employees didn't get a 401(k)-like option until 1986.

The Black Monday stock market crash in 1987 was so devastating to this segment of the population because the Boomers were at mid-career, and the changing laws and trends in retirement funding forced them to become their own investment advisors instead of being passive recipients of pension plans. They quite simply didn't have the knowledge, skills or time to manage their portfolios.

Here is the multi-faceted hard place:

- They were stuck with pension plans they could not access or influence;

- They had these new-fangled 401(k)s that they didn't really understand, and that had limited maximum contributions;

- They are living longer. Where once, most people did not even live long enough to reach full retirement age, now we live an average of 14 years past the age of 65 to age 79. In the simplest terms, this requires much more money.

"The baby boomers are the first group to face this new retirement era and have many challenges ahead of them, including the burden of saving and investing for up to 70% (*or more—my addition*) of their retirement, making those savings last for 20–30 years, and dealing with two of the worst economic environments in the history of investing (Internet & housing bubbles) during the most critical time for them to build their retirement savings," wrote Robert Laura in *Forbes* on Sept. 30, 2013.

That's frightening enough in itself.

Laura concludes, "Quite frankly, it's surprising the group is not further behind or hasn't completely given up. It's no wonder people avoid talking about retirement because everything they read, see and hear is designed to scare them or make them feel bad about being behind. The reality is, this is not your parents' or grandparents' retirement and people are behind and concerned for very real reasons."

I saw the devastation of Black Monday. One client referred to me at that time was a steel company retiree from Gary, IN. When the company went bankrupt, his pension stopped abruptly. It took a little time, but the Pension Benefit Guaranty Corporation did eventually make good on some of the lost benefits, but not all of them. In the interim, my client had no choice but to dip into savings that he knew he couldn't replace.

Thousands of retirees were in the same sinking boat.

But it's not all dismal. I have to add a few words of encouragement here: Yes, there are reasons, lots of good reasons, why you may be behind in preparing for retirement, saving the money you will need to maintain your current lifestyle, to travel and enjoy life. We can reverse course and help get you on track for the retirement you've always envisioned, even if you need to work a few years beyond typical retirement age.

I know it's stressful to think about all of these things. When typical retirement plans morphed from company-managed pension plans, where no employee decisions were necessary or even allowed, to the modern-day 401(k)s, workers were transformed overnight into becoming their own financial advisors, expected to make investment choices that would dramatically affect the rest of our lives. Many of us didn't do too well in that new role.

You don't need to make jokes about working until you're 150 years old or worry incessantly about the future if you should become ill.

Yes, it will take some work, a little penny pinching as you increase your contributions to your retirement funds, wise investing decisions and a hands-on approach.

This book is not just about money. It's about your life. Yes, money is a part of it, but it's also about family, living, health and enjoyment.

Stay with me; I'll show you how. We can do this together.

CHAPTER 2

Aging Gracefully

Every day, each of us gets older. Aging is inevitable. Considering the alternative, that's a good thing!

None of us want to think of ourselves as elderly, hunch-backed, creeping along with a walker or in a wheelchair, mentally compromised and a burden to our children. Now is the time to ask yourself the question, "Do you consider yourself to be a burden or a resource?"

This is the time in your life when you can have some control over that question and you can make the choices that will give you the vibrant health you want.

We're living longer. A man turning 65 today can expect to live, on average, until age 84 and a woman to age 86, according to the Social Security Administration. About one in every four 65-year-olds today will live past age 90 and one in ten will live past 95.

Within ten years, the website Global Age Watch (www.helpage.org) estimates that there will be one billion elderly people worldwide. An aging population is changing societies and their priorities throughout the world.

The good news: We are staying healthy much later in life than our parents or our grandparents. At 65 and beyond, many, if not most of us are healthy and strong. We're hiking the Appalachian Trail, playing tennis, river rafting in the Rockies and scuba diving in Cozumel.

The bad news: While most of us would dearly love to go to bed one night at the age of 99 and simply not wake up in the morning, this rarely happens. The human body does break down. Illness happens. The body becomes debilitated. Death is inevitable.

Why am I talking about physical and mental health in this book? This is a book about *fiscal* health, right?

Here's why: Your physical health is a very big part of your fiscal health. Illness is expensive in every aspect of life. It is stressful. It is emotionally debilitating. It is painful. And, yes, it will drain your bank account. So staying healthy is a primary element of any retirement plan.

Our health is also a part of general well-being and a sense of personal security. Global Age Watch places the well-being of seniors in the United States number 8 in the world, but we rank far below other developed countries at #36 in income security for elderly people, #24 for health status and #16 for living in an enabling environment. All of these stressors take a toll on our health, as you'll see in the next section

Manage stress

Stress is the underlying cause of a great deal of illness. The American Psychological Association estimates that 75 to 90% of all visits to the doctors are for stress-related ailments and complaints. Adverse health effects of stress include headaches, high blood pressure, heart disease, diabetes, skin conditions, cognitive dysfunction, obesity, asthma, arthritis, depression, anxiety, and perhaps even some forms of cancer. At least 43% of us suffer health problems directly related to stress.

How often do you lie awake at night worrying about bills, the possible loss of a job, your health or your spouse's health, or whether you'll ever have enough money to retire comfortably? Insomnia is one of the many manifestations of stress.

Getting ready to retire and worrying you won't have enough is stressful. For younger generations, it's stressful just to think about the ever-moving goalpost of retirement.

We all have stress. It's a natural part of life. Not all stress is linked to negative life events. The birth of a new grandchild or a new job can be just as stressful as moving to a different state or becoming ill.

It's not just the presence of stress that damages health, it's how we handle stress. Think of a caveman who was chased by a saber-toothed tiger: His entire survival mechanism kicked into hyperdrive. Our bodies are hard-wired to survive and so were those of our ancestors. But the caveman had the good sense, unlike modern humans, to kick back and relax and let off the steam once the emergency had passed and the saber-toothed tiger had been evaded for another day. Today's humans stay in physical stress mode most of the time, running from traffic jams to office meetings to speeding tickets to picking up kids at day care, hurried meal prep, homework, arguments with spouses, unfolded laundry and on and on and on. Unrelieved stress and the constant flow of the stress hormones cortisol and adrenaline translate into health challenges.

The Occupational Safety and Health Administration (OSHA) has declared stress a hazard of the workplace that costs American industry more than $300 billion annually.

So managing stress is a key element of staving off the most ravaging effects of aging. There are lots of excellent books about stress management. I recommend that you buy one or two and use them in your life.

> *Do not try to live forever; you will not succeed.*
> —George Bernard Shaw

Healthy diet

I don't need to go through all of the research that confirms that a diet rich in vegetables, fruit, lean meats and healthy fats can prevent the dread diseases of aging: heart disease, cancer, diabetes, obesity and Alzheimer's.

The Standard American Diet (SAD for short) is heavy on sugar, processed foods and simple carbohydrates. It is a health destroyer.

If you lunch frequently at fast food restaurants and chow down on greasy burgers, mounds of fries and wash them down with sugary soft drinks, you're well on your way to serious health problems.

If you'd rather put a frozen dinner in the oven than make a salad for dinner, you're on your way to serious health problems.

If you think catsup is a vegetable, you probably already have a serious health problem.

When your doctor admonishes you to "eat less and exercise more," while discreetly adjusting his white coat across his own spreading waistline, you'd be quite right to question how much he really knows about health.

You can make your own choices, but science shows us several ways to eat to live a longer and healthier life:

1. **Avoid almost all types of sugar.** This includes soft drinks, baked goods and other products sweetened with sugar and high fructose corn syrup that are quietly added in unexpected places like in commercial spaghetti sauces. This includes artificial sweeteners, which have been shown to cause insulin spikes, leading to or increasing insulin resistance characteristic of diabetes.

2. **Avoid processed foods.** Anything in a box or can is likely to be highly processed and contained additives, excess sodium, genetically modified organisms and other substances proven to be hazardous to your health.

3. **Eat as many vegetables as you possibly can.** Five servings a day is OK, nine or ten is even better. This can include one or two servings of fruit. A huge volume of research shows that people who eat the most vegetables live longer and have the lowest risk of chronic disease.

4. **Eat a Mediterranean diet** that includes lots of fish, veggies, olive oil, nuts, whole grains and a little bit of wine. This diet has been study-proven time and time again to be among the healthiest ways to maintain a healthy weight and prevent cancer and Alzheimer's.

5. **For some, decreasing gluten** (found in all wheat products) intake or eliminating it entirely is proving to be a powerful way of reducing belly fat, which places all of us at high risk of diabetes, obesity and heart disease.

We're all looking for ways to make the aging process easier and to stay healthy far into our later years. Truth to be told, most of think we will always be healthy and strong. None of us think we'll age the way we have seen our parents and family members age. We have the ability to make the right food choices to extend our lives.

Beautiful young people are accidents of nature,
but beautiful old people are works of art.
—Eleanor Roosevelt

Exercise

I think exercise is often a dreaded word as we grow older. It doesn't have to be. And it doesn't mean you have to spend hours at the gym or learn to play tennis when it is the last thing you want to do.

At the same time, exercise is a key element of physical and mental health. The entire body benefits from regular exercise. It helps control weight. It strengthens your heart, and even reverses some heart conditions and lowers blood pressure. It boosts energy and elevates mood, promotes better sleep, and even puts a spark back into your sex life!

Find a form of exercise you enjoy. In fact, find a form that you love. If you love it, you're much more likely to stick with an exercise program.

For many of us, it's something as simple as taking a vigorous 20-minute walk every day. Research shows this one simple form of exercise alone can cut the risk of heart disease in women by 40%. It can also extend your life rather dramatically. Retired men who walked less than one mile per day had mortality rates twice that of men who walked more than two miles per day, according to a 1998 study in the *New England Journal of Medicine*.

Almost everyone can walk. There's no special training, no special place you have to go. It doesn't require a partner, although it is nice to have someone to share your walks, and the only equipment you need is a decent pair of shoes. Best of all, it's free and you can do it anytime you like!

For those who live in climates where the weather is severe, there are even organized mall walking groups, eliminating the worries of slipping on icy sidewalks.

Some choose to wear a pedometer and aim for 10,000 steps a day. That may sound like a lot—it's about 4 miles for most stride lengths—but you'll probably be surprised how many steps you take in the ordinary course of your day, walking around the house, going to the supermarket, etc.

Of course, walking isn't the only form of exercise, but it's probably easiest.

Many seniors are now turning to mountain biking in my area. Others love swimming and attend water aerobics classes at the local pool.

Yoga is an excellent form of exercise at any age, for its physical benefits as well as it stress-relieving qualities.

It's important to be active. Research shows that couch potatoes dramatically shorten their lifespans.

It really doesn't matter what form of exercise you choose, just choose one and stick with it. It takes about three weeks to form a new habit, so grit your teeth and stick to your exercise program for at least three weeks. If, after that amount of time, it's still a struggle, find another form of exercise. More likely, you'll find you really miss your exercise time even if you take a break for a day.

Drop the "butt" habit

You've already heard it, but it's worth repeating here: Drop life-threatening habits and you will not only live longer, you'll live healthier.

Number one on this list is to stop smoking. Doctors say smoking is the single most health destroying habit anyone can indulge in. You already know that smoking causes lung cancer. It also causes heart disease and osteoporosis.

This U.S. Surgeon General's timeline may help inspire you as it has done for so many:

Within . . .	
20 minutes	heart rate and blood pressure drop
8 hours	nicotine in your system has dropped by 93.75%
10 days to 2 weeks	smoking is no long the uppermost in your mind
2 weeks to 3 months	heart attack risk has started to drop; lung function begins to improve
1 year	risk of heart disease, heart attack and stroke have dropped by 50%
10 years	risk of lung cancer has dropped by 30 to 50%

Smoking is one of the most difficult addictions to overcome. It's been said it is more difficult to stop smoking than to break a cocaine habit.

Fortunately, there are many types of smoking cessation drugs and support mechanisms available today to help ease that difficult journey. For some, the nicotine patches and gums work. For others, drugs like Wellbutrin (an anti-depressant), Chantix or Xyban to lessen nicotine cravings will ease you into becoming a non-smoker. The new e-cigarettes are very helpful for others.

Yes, it's difficult, but the results of giving up the habit are immediate and long lasting.

Brain health

Anyone who has known someone with dementia or its most common form, Alzheimer's disease, is well familiar with the terrible toll it takes.

A once-vibrant loved one slips away, sometimes with daunting personality changes. The disease is degenerative, meaning that there is no cure and it will become worse and worse over time until its victim's body literally "forgets" how to breathe.

Any of us who have seen the ugly face of Alzheimer's fear it will visit us, since we know there is a genetic component.

Even if we don't carry the dread APOE Alzheimer's gene, the risk of having Alzheimer's is now 1 in 9 for 65 year-olds. That risk rises to one in two, or a 50–50 chance you'll have it if you reach the age of 85, according to the Alzheimer's Association.

You can beat those odds with some simple lifestyle adjustments.

Not surprisingly, one of these is exercise. Regular exercisers cut their risk of Alzheimer's by nearly 50%, according to a 2006 study from the University of Washington published in the Annals of Internal Medicine.

Another is alcohol consumption, but maybe not the way you might guess. Those who are moderate alcohol consumers (1–2 drinks per day) dropped their Alzheimer's risk by nearly half over teetotalers, say researchers in the iconic Rotterdam study of nearly 8,000 seniors published in the British medical journal Lancet in 2002.

You can't do much now about your years of education—or can you?

Studies show that those who have less than eight years of formal education had nearly double the risk of Alzheimer's than those who completed high school.

These numbers mean less about intelligence than about the lifelong use of brainpower. Numerous studies show that people who are the most intellectually engaged in life and committed to lifelong learning have a lower risk of Alzheimer's.

This is the time to take the old admonition, "Use it or lose it," to heart—or to your brain. Take a class at your community college, learn how to use a computer or a new operating system, or try to learn a language (studies show you don't actually have to *learn* it, you just have to use your brain to try). Join a book club, do sudoku or crossword puzzles. Write a journal.

I just recently joined an online brain training program that is really fun as well as challenging. It's part of my personal commitment to preserving my brainpower. I urge you to find something similar and commit to it on a daily basis.

The possibilities are as endless as your exercise options. Just find something you love and stick with it.

Enjoy friends and family

Having a strong social network (and I don't mean an electronic one) is a ticket to a healthier and less stressful life.

In fact, having strong ties to family and friends and an active social life reduced the odds of dying from any cause by 50% over a 7.5-year study period, according to a mega-study of over 300,000 people from Brigham Young University and the University of North Carolina at Chapel Hill. Researchers noted that the reduced mortality for a solid friends network is quite similar to the decreased chances of death when you stop smoking.

Part of the protection for social networks seems to be from enhanced immune systems. In a classic 2003 study, Carnegie Mellon researchers reported that people with a wide diversity of social relationship were significantly less likely to develop a cold.

And on the other side of the coin, people who reported they were lonely, especially men, were far more likely to die of heart disease than those who had happy friend and family networks.

Loneliness is a particular concern for those who are widowed or whose families are far away. For your own health, even if it is a bit of a stretch for you, get out and socialize. If you don't have a lot of friends, make some. There are endless ways to make friends through churches, gyms, book clubs, hiking groups and senior centers.

Volunteerism is another health booster and an excellent way to meet people who share your community-minded interests.

Laugh a lot

Before I finish this section on social relationships and the chapter on health, I want to add the value of laughter to the longevity list.

There's a landmark scientific study from Denmark, where researchers studied 54,000 people over a 7-year period. Those who laughed the most had a 35% greater chance of being alive after seven years than sourpusses.

Even more exciting, cancer patients in the Danish study lived 70% longer if they laughed more.

You've probably heard the story of magazine editor Norman Cousins, who was diagnosed with a painful and life-threatening form of arthritis called ankylosing spondylitis in 1976. Doctors told Cousins he had six months to live and that there was little they could do to relieve his intense pain. So he checked himself out of the hospital and into a hotel room, where he took mega-doses of vitamin C and created his own personal video marathon of Marx Brothers films and TV sitcoms.

Cousins quickly discovered that ten minutes of belly laughter allowed him two hours of pain-free sleep—relief he couldn't even get from morphine. Over time, with continued laughter therapy and a positive attitude, Cousins' disease disappeared. He died of unrelated causes 14 years later at the age of 75.

Cousins' story is an inspiration to us all.

So the take-home message of this chapter is to live long and healthy with the right food, the right exercise, the right friends and lots of laughter.

CHAPTER 3

Fiscal Fitness Matters

Jonathan Clement, the noted English financial writer, once wisely said, "Retirement is like a long vacation in Las Vegas. The goal is to enjoy yourself to the fullest, but not so fully that you run out of money." Of course, that presumes you saved something for retirement in the first place!
—Duke Woodhall, a friend of mine

So, how much income do you think you will need in retirement?

Here's where my contrarian thinking comes into play. I'm going to tell you that you need 100% to 120% of your current take home pay at the time you retire and for your first 10 to 15 years in retirement.

In simple terms, this means if your net is $60,000 a year, you will need between $60,000 and $72,000 to maintain your current lifestyle.

That doesn't include inflation, which I like to factor at 2% a year right now.

Are you a little surprised? Most retirement calculators will tell you that you need 70 to 80% of your current net income. Why do I think you will need to so much more? It's simple: We're living longer and we need to have money to last longer.

I've mentioned these figures before, but they bear repeating here: A man turning 65 today can expect to live, on average, until age 84 and a woman to age 86, according to the Social Security Administration. About one in every four 65-year olds today will live past age 90, and one in ten will live past 95.

You could easily live 20 to 30 years beyond retirement.

If you retired 30 years ago in 1984 and you were lucky enough to be alive today, you'd probably be giving yourself apoplexy over the prices.

> *The future ain't what it use to be.*
> —YOGI BERRA

Take a look at the figures in the box below and you'll see why you need money to retire—and lots of it.

How much will it cost?

Times change quickly. You could easily live 30 years after retirement. So imagine you retired 30 years ago today. How would you be living in 2014? Look at these comparisons:

Average income:
1984: $21,600
Today: $69,821

Average Social Security income:
1984: $314
Today: $1,230

The average house:
1984: $79,900
Today: $168,261

Average rent:
1984: $350
Today: $1,008

New car:
1984: $8,995
Today: $30,303

Gallon of gas:
1984: $1.10
Today: $3.60

Cornflakes
1984: 89 cents
Today: $3.79

Pound of hamburger:
1984: $1.29
Today: $4.11

Gallon of milk:
1984: $2.26
Today: $3.43

Big Mac:
1984: $1.50
Today: $4.56

Postage Stamp:
1984: 20 cents
Today: 46 cents

Average cost of one-night hospital stay:
1984: $800
Today: $1,760

A nickel ain't worth a dime anymore.

—YOGI BERRA

Now imagine that you retired today. What do you think prices might look like in 30 years, when there is a fair chance you'll still be alive?

Today's retirees are living longer than those of previous generations. When the Social Security Act became law in 1935, the average life expectancy was 61.7 years. That meant a significant proportion of the population never even reached the age where they would be eligible to collect benefits.

Today's retirees can expect to live to age 79—17.3 years longer. Not only does that mean that Social Security will have to pay benefits for much longer, hence the strain on the Social Security system, but that the current generation of retirees will have to support themselves much longer.

What's your vision?

How do you envision your retirement? Do you think of yourself trekking in the Himalayas? Strolling the Champs Elysees? On safari in Africa?

Or are you relishing the thought of spending time in your garden, rocking on your front porch and occasionally entertaining the grandkids?

The retirement income you'll need is directly related to your plans. Sometimes plans have to be modified or reined in a bit as the reality of life without a paycheck settles in.

If you're still working, congratulations on getting to this subject *before* you get into full-blown panic mode.

So let's go back to the question I posed at the beginning of this book: How important is money to you?

YOUR FINANCIAL PROFILE

Let's get started with a basic worksheet that will help you and your financial advisor assess your current financial status, your goals and your needs in retirement.

Personal Information

Full Name:_____   Date of Birth: _____

Projected retirement date: _____   Gross annual income: _____

Spouse: _____

Date of Birth: _____   Projected retirement date: _____

Gross annual income: _____   Former spouse: _____

Financial advisor: _____

Address:_____   Phone:_____

Do you give to charities?   ❑ YES   ❑ NO

Which ones? _____

_____

Do you expect an inheritance
or other income?   ❑ YES   ❑ NO   ❑ Maybe   Amount: $_____

Assets and Liabilities

Name	Total Value	Debt
Residence	$_____	$_____
Real Estate	$_____	$_____
Other Assets	$_____	
Other Liabilities (credit card, etc)	$_____	
Collectibles	$_____	
Limited Partnership	$_____	$_____
Business	$_____	$_____

Cash, Checking	$_____
Savings, CDs, T-Bills	$_____
Bonds / Fixed Income	$_____
Annuities	$_____
Stocks / Mutual Funds	$_____
TOTAL ASSETS	$_____
TOTAL LIABILITIES	$_____
YOUR NET WORTH	$_____

Retirement Plan	Total Value	Monthly Savings	Company Match
401k	$_____	$_____	_____%
IRA	$_____	$_____	_____%
Roth IRA	$_____	$_____	_____%
Simple IRA	$_____	$_____	_____%
Pension	$_____	$_____	_____%

Income (Monthly)

Wages and Bonuses (Take-home pay)	$_____
Wages and Bonuses (spouse)	$_____
Miscellaneous Income (describe:)	$_____
TOTAL CURRENT INCOME:	$_____

Social Security Income (Projected or Actual)

	Before Age 62	Before Age 66	Before Age 70
Your Monthly income	$_____	$_____	$_____
Spouse's Monthly income	$_____	$_____	$_____
TOTAL SOCIAL SECURITY	$_____		
(+) Monthly income	$_____	X 110% =	

WHAT YOU WILL NEED PER MONTH IN RETIREMENT $_____

Post-Retirement Expenses

Giving $_____

Savings $_____

Debt Repayment (Not home and car) $_____

Mortgage or Rent $_____

Homeowners Insurance / Property Taxes $_____

Home Repairs / Maintenance / HOA Dues $_____

Electricity / Water / Gas / Trash $_____

Phone (cell / land line) $_____

Car Payment(s) $_____

Gas / Car Repair / Maintenance / Oil $_____

Car Insurance $_____

Food (groceries) $_____

Entertainment (restaurant, etc.) $_____

Life / Disability / Long-Term Care Insurance $_____

Health Insurance / All Medical $_____

Child Care $_____

Clothes; Hygiene $_____

Miscellaneous Expenses $_____

TOTAL EXPENSES $_____

CURRENT TOTAL INCOME (from previous page) $_____

(–) TOTAL EXPENSES (from above) $_____

(=) NET MONTHLY CASH FLOW $_____
    (Total income minus expenses)

Rule of 72

If you're feeling a little glum after running these numbers, take heart. There are some ways of increasing your wealth rather quickly. Compounding interest is nothing short of miraculous.

Simply put, the Rule of 72 helps you determine how long it will take for your investment to double in value given a fixed annual rate of interest. That is because the interest, which you roll back into your original investment, begins to escalate the value of your investment dramatically. It's called compounding interest.

Here's an easy chart:

RULE OF 72	
RATE OF RETURN	RULE OF 72 YEARS
2%	36.0 years
3%	24.0 years
5%	14.4 years
7%	10.3 years
9%	8.0 years
12%	6.0 years

If you want to estimate how long it will take to double your money, take the number 72 and divide that number by the interest rate you are getting. So if you deposit $3,000 into an account with a 2% interest rate, 72 ÷ 2 is 36. So in 36 years you would have $6,000.

$$72 \div 2 = 36$$

If you have an interest rate of 12%, your investment would double in just six years. The higher the interest, the quicker you can double your money.

Here's a pretty compelling example of the Rule of 72:

Tim and Sue took different approaches to retirement savings:

Tim joined his company's 401(k) at age 25. He contributed $2,000 each year ($167 a month) for the next ten years, and then never contributed another penny to his retirement account.

Sue joined her company's 401(k) at age 35 and contributed $2,000 a year for the next 30 years.

Both earned 8% on their contributions and retired at age 65.

Who had more money at retirement? You'll be surprised at the answer:

Tim was the winner, by far. His contributions of $20,000 yielded a portfolio that was worth $314,870 at retirement and Sue's contribution of $60,000 had only grown to $244,693.

And of course, if Tim had continued funding his retirement for another 30 years, he would have been a multi-millionaire.

Compounding interest is the 8th wonder of the world!
—ALBERT EINSTEIN

The Rule of 72 is an approximation and is based on compounding a fixed rate of return over a long period of time. However, most investments generate fluctuating returns, so the period of time in which an investment can double cannot be determined with certainty. This is as hypothetical example and is not intended to represent an actual investment. This example does not consider any costs associated with investing. Both the principal and returns of investments vary over time. You may incur a profit or loss. Seeking higher rates of return involves greater risk.

So, OK, you're far behind in your savings plan. It's going to take some belt tightening, but a good financial planner can help you shape your retirement years by maximizing the returns from your current investments and helping you devise a plan to increase the amount you contribute to your retirement portfolio.

The three-legged stool

Retirement is a three-legged stool. Social Security was never meant to fund your retirement. It is only one leg of a stool, a stool that cannot stand unless you have two-thirds of your needs in other types of funds, including retirement funds, investments and personal savings.

I can't stress enough how important it is to make those three work together.

We'll go into detail on each of the three legs:

- Social Security

- Retirement plan (401(k)s, IRAs and pensions)

- Personal savings and investments

Social Security

Social Security is a major component of our retirement system. Between now and 2030, 72 million Americans born between 1946 and 1964 will become eligible for benefits.

You have many Social Security options, and your financial planner will help you figure out what is best for you. If you are married, there are some rather tricky waters that can easily be navigated with professional help that will maximize the surviving spouse's benefits in the case of the death of one partner.

As an aside, Social Security and Medicare are two entirely different programs. Regardless of your Social Security status or whether or not you are receiving Social Security benefits, you become eligible for Medicare at age 65.

In order to collect Social Security, you must have worked ten years in most cases.

Here's a very simple primer on Social Security:

DETERMINE YOUR FULL RETIREMENT AGE (FRA): This is the age at which you become eligible for full and unrestricted benefits, based on your date of birth. Currently FRA is 66 years, and in the coming years, it will gradually edge upward to 67 years by 2026.

EARLY BENEFITS CLAIMS: You can claim Social Security benefits as early as age 62, but there are substantial penalties involved. The reduction in benefits is calculated by the number of months between the filing date and your full retirement age (FRA). For example, if your FRA is 66 and you file at age 62, your benefits will be reduced by 25% for the remainder of your life.

There are additional restrictions on the amount of money you can earn without further benefits reduction if you file before your FRA. Until your reach your FRA, in 2013 you would lose $1 in benefits for every $2 in earnings above $15,120. If you reached your FRA in 2013, the income restriction goes up to $40,080, after which you would lose $1 for every $3 in earnings over that amount. After you reach your FRA, there is no limit to earnings if you took early retirement.

Early retirement may be necessary if you have an intensely physical job or a chronic illness, but in most cases, it's best to wait as long as you can before you begin collecting benefits.

FULL RETIREMENT AGE (FRA): When you reach full retirement age, your benefits will be calculated based on your earnings for your 35 highest earning years. If you are married and didn't work long enough to get a good benefit, you can retire at age 66 with half of your spouse's full benefit. Divorced spouses who were married at least ten years and have not remarried can collect benefits on their ex's account.

AGE TO RECEIVE FULL SOCIAL SECURITY BENEFITS

YEAR OF BIRTH*	FULL RETIREMENT AGE
1937 or earlier	65
1938	65 and 2 months
1939	65 and 4 months
1940	65 and 6 months
1941	65 and 8 months
1942	65 and 10 months
1943–1954	66
1955	66 and 2 months
1956	66 and 4 months
1957	66 and 6 months
1958	66 and 8 months
1959	66 and 10 months
1960 and later	67

* If you were born on January 1st of any year, you should refer to the previous year. If you were born on the 1st of the month, your benefit and your full retirement age are calculated as if your birthday was in the previous month.

DELAYED BENEFITS: You can file for Social Security any time from your 62nd birthday through your 70th birthday. The longer you wait, the higher your benefits will be, if you can wait.

In fact, if you wait until your 70th birthday to claim your benefits, you'll get an additional 8% in increased benefits when you begin receiving payments for each of the four years between ages 66 and 70. (Benefits will not increase after age 70.)

In other words, it's a no-brainer that you should wait as long as possible, if you can, to collect your benefit, unless, for some reason, you are certain you won't live to a ripe old age.

There are some complicated strategies that involve filing for benefits at FRA and suspending to help protect survivor benefits if one spouse had a very low income, but I'll leave that for you and your financial planner to determine.

INCREASE FOR DELAYED RETIREMENT TO AGE 70

YEAR OF BIRTH*	YEARLY RATE OF INCREASE	MONTHLY RATE OF INCREASE
1933–1934	5.5%	11/24 of 1%
1935–1936	6.0%	1/2 of 1%
1937–1938	6.5%	13/24 of 1%
1939–1940	7.0%	7/12 of 1%
1941–1942	7.5%	5/8 of 1%
1943 or later	8.0%	2/3 of 1%

*If you were born on January 1st of any year, you should refer to the previous year.

SURVIVOR BENEFITS: Many people have the erroneous notion that they'll keep getting their spouse's full benefits even after his/her death. That is not true. Social Security benefits stop upon death. In most cases, the surviving spouse will continue to receive the higher benefits, so, for example, if your spouse's benefits were $2,800 a month and yours were $2,000 a month, if he dies before you, in most cases, you will receive $2,800 a month until your death. This is an essential part of retirement planning. In this example, could you live on $2,000 a month less if your spouse dies? Your living expenses might be somewhat less, but would you be able to maintain your home?

How can you be sure you'll get your Social Security benefits? You can't be 100% sure, that's why we have the three-legged stool. However, the trustees of the Social Security fund say the current reserves will pay full benefits with cost-of-living increases through 2033 and tax income will cover 73% of promised benefits from 2036 through 2085, even if nothing changes. That means most of us have nothing to worry about.

Our kids and grandkids are likely to find the system changing, with later retirement ages, increased taxes, lowered benefits and lower cost-of-living adjustments.

Retirement accounts

Many of you probably worked for some years for companies that provided pension plans and then for companies that offered 401(k) plans. If you were self-employed or had no retirement plans offered through your employer, you may have had an IRA or a SEP IRA or Roth IRA.

You may have become confused or frustrated and thrown up your hands in despair and allowed the 401(k) plan representative to help you make a choice without any idea whether it was the right choice.

That may also leave you with a confusing portfolio of retirement investments. If you're like millions of Americans, you probably don't have any idea what's in your portfolio, why you're holding it or even how much it is worth today.

If you're like many, or even most of us, you don't think you know anything about investing and you don't want to get involved. Am I right?

Hopefully, you have a few—or a lot of—years left until retirement and you can maximize your financial potential with the help of your financial planner.

Here's a little bit of myth busting: Your financial planner can help you manage the funds inside your 401(k) as well as all types of IRAs. Whatever type of 401(k) plan your employer offers, you have a right to manage the funds within the plan and your financial planner is well-equipped to do so.

Personal savings and investments

I hope it's not too late to tell you this, but here goes: The earlier you start, the easier it is to save for retirement.

In a perfect world, children would begin saving a portion of their allowances and just keep on adding to that throughout their lifetimes.

I remember when I was 6 and I'd clutch my little red savings account book for my regular trips to the bank with my parents. I started my account with $5 and was thrilled to watch it grow as each deposit and interest earned was recorded.

The Boomers' parents were pretty good at saving for the future. Boomers aren't as good and the generations behind them are even worse at planning ahead.

I know, 20-somethings these days frequently don't even have jobs, much less are they even thinking about saving for retirement. Even in their 30s, young people are frequently more preoccupied with kids and jobs than thinking 30-plus years into the future.

The best way to predict the future is to invent it.
—ALAN KAY, COMPUTER SCIENTIST

But it's so much easier if they do. In fact, tell your kids and grandkids that accumulating enough money for retirement is easier if they start early enough.

It's also inevitably going to take some risk. What you and your financial planner will discover is how much tolerance you have to risk.

Risk

There are several types of risk and we need to consider them all as we develop our retirement plan.

Inflation is far and above the most important risk for retirees. It is something we cannot control. Inflation happens—like death and taxes—so we must factor cost of living increases into our fiscal fitness plans.

Risk is a part of God's game, alike for men and nations.
—WARREN BUFFET

The consumer price index shows us that the cost of living has increased 225% since 1984. Perhaps a more realistic figure shows a 24% increase in the past ten years and 58% in the last 20 years.

Again, I'm guessing most of you intend to be alive in ten years. Can you handle it if prices increase 24% or more? How about in 20 years?

Other types of risk include:

- **Market risk.** The risk that the stock market will go down, which it inevitably will from time to time. When we talk about risk tolerance, we're usually talking about our willingness to risk our principal in order to increase its value.

- **Political risk.** The risk that government policies will negatively affect the economy and your personal pocketbook.

- **Environmental risk.** The risk of environmental catastrophes, like the Gulf oil spill, Hurricane Katrina or Tropical Storm Sandy, and their impact on certain geographical areas.

- **Interest rate risk.** Interest rates fluctuate over time. In the early 1970s when I bought my first house with a 10.5% mortgage, I never in my wildest dreams would have imagined that mortgage rates would drop to today's historic lows of around 3%.

A big part of my job as a financial advisor is to prepare you for the day you receive your last paycheck. I'm the first to tell you, I've seen high-ranking executives of Fortune 500 companies cry when that last paycheck was finally in their hands. No matter how eagerly they have been anticipating retirement, there is a huge transition and a realization that the working portion of their lives has ended.

Not only do I help prepare clients for that transition, I help them replace that paycheck with income from their investment portfolios.

So there's a balance between risk and fear. I can tell you from my decades of experience that fear always overcomes greed. I've had clients tell me that they have a very high tolerance for risk, but when the stock market starts to slide, they go into high panic mode. They mean they can tolerate risk to *increase* their wealth, but they can't tolerate risk if that same wealth starts to shrink.

Sadly, that's not the way it works. High risk can result in huge gains or equally huge losses. Despite what they might say, most people cannot tolerate the idea of major losses in their portfolios.

Here's a simple diagram that shows emotional reactions I've witnessed as market conditions change:

Emotional Cycles of the Market

You've invested $100,000. The market starts to swing, as it usually does. This is how most people react.

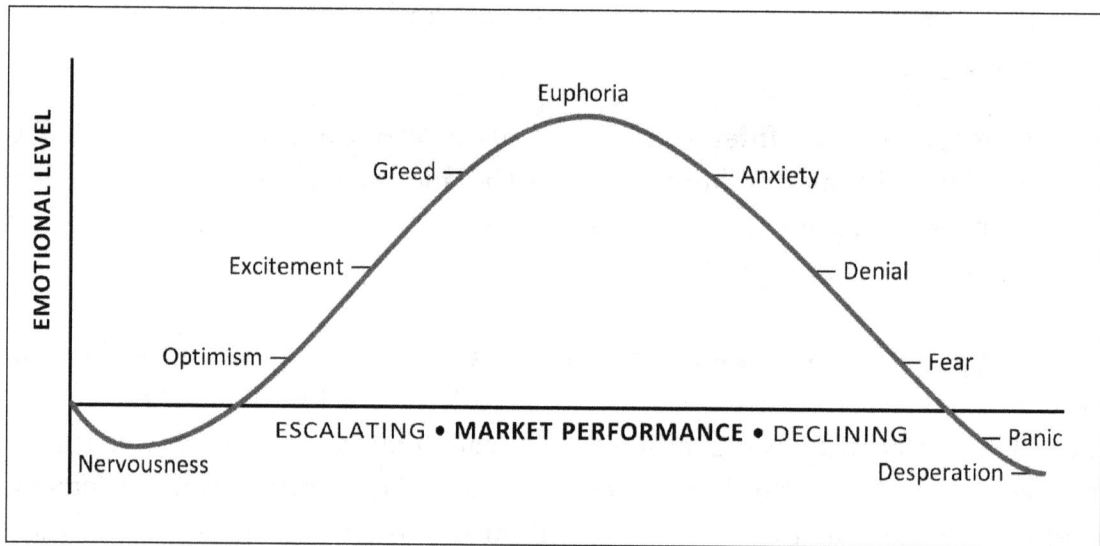

Emotional Cycles of the Market

I've told you before that I am considered somewhat of a contrarian thinker. There is the euphoria of a strong market when everybody else says, "Buy! Buy! Buy!"

That's exactly the wrong time to buy. Look at how many people suffered from the bursting dot-com bubble in the '90s and the housing bubble prior to the 2008 crash. The 2008 crash scared many people into their shells. That's why there is still so much cash on the sidelines six years later.

We never know how markets will respond to historic events, but the past has shown that major catastrophes may cause brief market downturns, but those losses are usually recouped fairly quickly. For example, the assassination of President John F. Kennedy on Nov. 22, 1963 caused a one-day stock market drop of 3%, but that was almost completely recovered within a week. The same was generally true of the beginning of World War II with the bombing of Pearl Harbor on Dec. 7, 1941. The Sept. 11 terrorist attacks in 2001 had dramatic, immediate effects when the market fell more than 7%, but those losses were recouped within a month.

How do you deal with the stresses of up and down markets?

I have a simple solution: Let your financial planner deal with it. Turn off the TV, stop listening to the talking heads, delete the scrolling stock ticker from your computer and enjoy your life.

Historically, the market has its highs and lows, but the trend has always been upward: Just note that the day before President Kennedy was assassinated, the Dow Jones Industrials stood at 732. As of this writing in October of 2013, the Dow stands at 15,687, nearly 15,000 points higher, far outpacing inflation and seemingly confirming the wisdom of the slow and steady "buy and hold" school of investment thought.

The Dow Jones Industrial Average is an unmanaged index of common stock that tracks changes in stock prices of the 30 most significant and commonly traded U.S. industrial stocks on the New York Stock Exchange. Investors cannot invest in unmanaged indices, but there are index funds based on the Dow Jones Industrial Average that can be purchased. All economic and performance data is historical and not indicative of future results. Please keep in mind that no investment strategy can assure a profit or protect against loss in declining markets.

So, if you simply don't have the money you need to retire, and you're too close to retirement for the potential returns to make much difference right now, the alternative is to save more.

Here's a simple example:

Julie is 50 years old with a gross income of $100,000.

She needs $60,000 a year (her take-home pay) in retirement.

Figuring 2% inflation and a 5% rate of return after taxes for the next 30 years, she needs $1.25 million going into retirement.

With no retirement savings at all, she would have to save 32% of her gross income today until retirement in order to make her goal.

That would seriously cramp her lifestyle.

But Julie does have some retirement savings, about $300,000. That cuts savings needs to about 21% of her gross income. It is still a stretch to save $1,750 a month, but at her income level, it is possible and Julie is very motivated.

And because she is healthy and loves her job, there's every reason to believe she can work until age 70 or more, so her comfort level and hedges against inflation can be increased with every year she works and stashes away that 21% toward retirement.

Investment opportunities

There are innumerable ways to invest your money. Part of the process is your faith and trust in your financial planner, who will help you formulate an investment strategy that is comfortable for you. If you're incessantly worrying about your money, it's time to consider a less aggressive investment strategy, and perhaps to scale back your expectations.

Risk comes from not knowing what you are doing.
—WARREN BUFFETT

A good financial planner will never put all of your nest egg in one basket. Your portfolio should be what we call "diversified," which means it invests in a broad variety of investments across various sectors, including mutual funds, stocks, real estate investment trusts and bonds.

As an interesting aside, the 2013 Nobel prize in economics went to Gene Fama and Lars Hansen of the University of Chicago and Robert Schiller of Yale for very different opinions about the ways to predict market prices over the long term.

What is a financial planner?

In the simplest terms, financial planners advise their clients on how to save, invest and manage their money in order to meet their life goals. A good financial planner can give you advice about retirement plans, insurance, Social Security, real estate, estate planning and just about anything related to your money.

A financial planner helps you identify what you want to do when you grow up. She'll help you define your values, take the time to learn what is important in your life and help you build a roadmap to achieve those goals.

Many people think a financial planner just handles investments, but that's not the case. In fact, I think we are more like life planners. We look at the big picture, listen to your plans and help you realize your dreams.

I actually like to work with the clients and meet with them and their lawyers and accountants to make sure that we are all moving in the same direction.

Another aspect of our work is what I call *legacy planning*. This is a major area where we financial planners are so much more than just investment advisors.

In my mind, wealth is more than worldly possessions. I'm not talking about wills or estate planning. I'm talking about the legacy you want to leave when you're gone. Legacy planning helps my clients express and record family values and traditions, charitable giving, personal and medical histories that may help future generations, final wishes and even personal messages they want to leave for loved ones.

I've included more about legacy planning in Chapters 5 and 6.

How should I choose a financial planner?

Trust is the most important aspect in a relationship with a financial planner. Do you like him or her? Would you want to socialize with her, go out to dinner with him? Or are you eager to escape after every meeting? These are good indicators. Trust your gut. If the relationship doesn't feel comfortable, it won't be comfortable a year or ten years or 20 years down the road.

Look for a recognized designation such as Chartered Financial Consultant (ChFC) or Certified Financial Planner (CFP). It means this professional has passed a rigorous test about the specifics of personal finance and is committed to continuing education.

Ask your friends. Word-of-mouth is the most common way of finding a financial planner with whom you'll be happy.

Make an appointment. Ask questions: How long have you been in business? What is the average age of your clients? How many of them are retirees? How many assets do you have under management?

Be prepared to answer lots of questions from your prospective planner to help tailor recommendations for you.

Talk to more than one candidate.

If you are part of a couple, be aware that most planners insist on talking to both members of the couple together so that everyone gets on the same page about retirement decisions.

If you're a woman (and women make 80% of all buying decisions), does your planner treat you respectfully and talk directly to you, not down to you? Again, you must feel comfortable with your planner.

Later, if you feel less comfortable with your choice, feel free to change your planner.

CHAPTER 4

What You Need to Know About Insurance

Insurance is an assurance that you, your family and your assets are protected against all sorts of disasters, ranging from accidental injury to catastrophic illness to your premature death.

Insurance is an investment that gives peace of mind.

When we look at some of the daunting statistics, having Medicare and a good supplemental policy, long-term care insurance and life insurance makes sense for most people, except those with extremely high incomes.

Did you know that government statistics show:

- 37% of people requiring long-term care are between the ages of 18 and 64 and 70% of people who are 65 today will need long term care sometime in the future, according to the U.S. Centers for Medicare and Medicaid Services?

- The average cost of assisted living is $3,550 a month? *

- The average cost of a private room in a nursing home is more than $90,000 a year and escalating at a rate of 5 to 8% every year? *

- The average nursing home stay is 835 days? *

*Statistics reported in the 2012 U.S. government's Nursing Home Survey.

Here's the big news that very few people seem to understand:
Medicare and supplemental health insurance do not pay for long-term care!

It's easy to see how quickly a nursing home or assisted living stay can gobble up assets, sometimes leaving a spouse without sufficient assets to continue the lifestyle the couple so carefully planned earlier in life.

I am talking mainly to the senior population here, so I'll explore Medicare in some depth. Yes, younger people need medical insurance, too, and the Affordable Care Act is intended to broaden access to health insurance, but as of this writing, it remains to be seen how well that will work.

There are three basic types of insurance you should consider, based on the value of your portfolio, your age and your life circumstances:

- Medicare

- Long-term care insurance

- Life insurance

This book is meant to be a primer on these types of insurance. They are very complex with virtually unlimited permutations, but this will give you the basic information you need to start the process.

Medicare

Medicare is government-provided health insurance available to anyone 65 or older, certain younger people with disabilities and people with end-stage kidney disease.

Medicare comes in four parts:

PART A. Covers in-patient hospital stays. It almost never covers skilled nursing facilities. Hospice care and, in rare circumstances, some home health care may be covered.

PART B. Covers certain doctors' services, outpatient care, medical supplies and outpatient services.

PART C. Also known as Medicare Advantage plans, is an optional type of Medicare health plan offered by private companies that contract with Medicare to provide all of your Parts A and B benefits, sometimes charging an additional premium. Part C providers include HMOs, PPOs, private fee-for-service plans and a few others.

PART D. Prescription drug coverage offered by private companies approved by Medicare. Many Medicare Advantage plans also include Part D coverage. Otherwise, recipients can purchase Part D plans separately.

There is another type of Medicare insurance, sometimes called Medigap, but more commonly known as Medicare Supplement insurance. These policies help make up the costs that Medicare does not cover. Federal law requires standardization of plans for all Medigap policies, so it's easy to compare apples to apples when you're looking at policies offered by different companies.

Medicare covers quite a bit, but generally it's not enough.

If you have standard Medicare coverage, a Medicare supplemental policy is extremely important. If you have to pay out-of-pocket 20% of a $100,000 bill, the $20,000 co-pay could be problematic for many.

For example, in the calendar year 2014, you pay a maximum of $1,216 for hospital stays between 1 and 60 days. If you're hospitalized on Dec. 31, 2014, you'll pay the $1,216 in 2014 and if you're not released until sometime in January 2015, you'll pay an additional $1,216. It's complicated and expensive!

If you're in the hospital for a long time, you'll pay $30–40 *per day* for days 61 to 90. Beyond 90 days in the hospital, the formula become even more complicated, but basically, you'll be ponying up $608 a day out of pocket.

A maximum stay of 100 days in a skilled nursing facility is covered by Medicare *only* if you've been in a hospital for at least three days and a doctor has certified that you need skilled nursing care for rehabilitation purposes. It is *not* nursing home care.

For example, someone who has had a stroke or a joint replacement could be placed in a skilled nursing facility while recuperating and undergoing therapy for rehabilitation. In that case, Medicare pays for the first 20 days and for days 21–100, you'll pay $152 a day. Beyond day 100, you pay all costs, which you already know are substantial. And the facility will re-certify you, usually every 30 days, to confirm that you are making progress. If you are not making progress, Medicare will discontinue its payments. This happened to a cantankerous old man I knew who had broken his hip. He didn't like the rehab facility and he would not participate in physical therapy until he was warned that Medicare payments would be discontinued unless he was making progress.

As another example, someone who has late-stage cancer or Alzheimer's and is not expected to recover would not be a candidate for rehabilitation and, as you know, nursing home care expenses are not covered by Medicare.

Generally, Medicare will pay for hospice costs from a Medicare-approved provider, but with a lot of strings attached. However, Medicare does not pay for room and board for people who need hospice care.

Other items and services that Medicare doesn't cover include:

- Routine dental or eye care

- Dentures

- Cosmetic surgery

- Acupuncture

- Hearing aids and exams for fitting them

- Routine foot care

There are many organizations (some of them insurance companies with a vested interest) that will help Medicare recipients learn about their options.

State Health Insurance Assistance Programs (SHIP) provide counselors to help navigate the sometimes stormy Medicare waters. Information about your state's SHIP contact information is available at shiptalk.org.

There is also a wealth of information available at medicare.gov, including consumer ratings of companies offering Medicare Supplement plans.

Long-term care insurance

This is where you can protect yourself, your assets, your family and your legacy from being drained by the high cost of nursing home care or assisted living. With the right policy, you can also protect yourself from being forced into a nursing home if you'd prefer to stay at home, even in the case of a debilitating illness.

The cost of long-term care is the single largest contributor to financial ruin for seniors.

Most people would use up their savings within a year or two in a nursing home.

There are many reasons why you might choose to buy long-term care insurance, including:

- To protect your family by easing financial and emotional burdens that could be placed on your loved ones;

- To protect assets and life savings;

- To protect and preserve family inheritances;

- To remain independent and continue to make your own choices about care, home, doctors, etc.;

- To avoid depleting all of your estate and becoming dependent on public assistance;

- To buy it while you are healthy since you are likely to be denied coverage if you are ill or cognitively impaired;

- Concern that costs will increase in the future. You can be assured they will;

- You know someone who has needed long-term care.

Do you need long-term care insurance? If you have a net worth of less than $10 million, you want to choose the place you'll go if you need care, and you don't want to become dependent on your children, you need long-term care insurance. Otherwise, just skip this section and be prepared that you may need to write some large checks sometime in the future.

At the same time, you don't have to insure the whole amount of long-term care. Insure what you *can't* afford. If the cost of a skilled nursing facility in your community is $9,000 a month (that's about what it is where I live), and you can afford to pay $4,500 a month, then only buy long-term care insurance to cover $4,500. Remember, if you are in a nursing home, your spouse may still be healthy and you'll need to cover his/her living expenses, so consider that possibility in your calculation of what you can afford.

Did you know that:

- More than twice as many women need long-term care as men?

- Nearly half of those admitted to nursing homes will eventually end up on Medicaid (publicly funded care) because they have exhausted all of their assets?

- More than 80% of out-of-pocket medical expenses for elderly people go toward paying the cost of nursing home care?

- About one-third of all long-term care expenses are paid out-of-pocket by individual patients or their families?

- A 90-day nursing home stay would impoverish about 30% of the elderly unless they have insurance or another way to pay for their care?

* Statistics from the U.S. government 2012 Nursing Home Survey

Long-term care is defined as extended care often lasting a year or more. It provides skilled nursing care or rehabilitation either in a facility or at home; assistance with ADL (activities of daily living), that include bathing, showering, dressing, eating, walking, toileting and custodial care in the case of cognitive impairment, such as Alzheimer's disease.

Long-term care insurance should include:

- Help with ADL

- Home health care

- Respite care

- Adult day care

- Nursing home care

- Assisted living care

At one time, a dozen or more companies offered long-term care insurance. Today, only a handful of companies offer plans. Prices vary based on the type of policy you want and your age. I bought my long-term care policy when I was 50. The younger you are, in general, the lower the cost. At one time, lifetime benefit policies were available, but now the longest term available is 10 years. In that case, if you're in a nursing home or in need of home health care, the longest you might be able to collect benefits would be ten years.

Here's a primer on the benefits offered in long-term care policies and the choices you can make, including:

- **Types of covered facilities:** These can range from home care, independent living facilities and retirement communities with varying levels of care, to residential care, adult day care, assisted living and nursing homes.

- **Daily benefits:** This is the payment to you per day in a skilled nursing facility. These usually range between $50 and $300 per day.

- **Inflation protection:** This adjusts the daily benefit amount annually to protect against inflation. This can be a compounded or simple inflation rate. Be sure that you buy a policy with a compounded inflation rate. It will cost more, but it's worth it.

- **Benefit period:** The length of time the policy will pay for your care, usually from 2 to 5 years from the time you begin to use it.

- **Waiting period:** The number of days you must pay for your care before insurance coverage begins. This may range from 0 to 100 days. The longer the waiting period, the lower your premium.

- **Home health care coverage:** Allows a person to receive care at home for as long as possible.

- **Levels of care:** A good policy will cover all levels of nursing home care: skilled, intermediate and custodial.

- **Guaranteed renewable for life:** A key aspect of long-term care.

- **Other benefits:** There may be discounts for husband and wife coverage, and benefits from a spouse who dies may be applied to the surviving spouse. Policies should cover Alzheimer's disease and other forms of dementia.

This is a very complex form of insurance, and it's essential to have someone you trust to guide you through the process and ensure that you get what you need and what you want. If your financial advisor doesn't sell long-term care insurance (I don't), she can refer you to someone who does.

Life insurance

This is going to be a short section on a complex subject. Whether or not life insurance is appropriate for you is a fairly simple choice.

If you are of an age when you still have a mortgage, minor children or children in college, you need life insurance.

Life insurance for estate planning (largely to pay taxes on large inheritances) is a consideration for high asset clients.

A large part of the retired population doesn't need life insurance.

Here's a simple questionnaire to help you make the decision. Of course, you know by now, I'll recommend that decision be made with the advice of your financial advisor.

- Do you have a mortgage?

- Do you have minor children?

- Do you have kids in college?

- Do you have enough assets to cover your debts?

- Do you own farmland or high value property that is likely to incur substantial estate taxes? (Today's laws give a husband and wife a total of $10 million in value before estate taxes are collectible.)

If your answer to any of these questions is "yes," then by all means, get life insurance to cover your needs. But remember, as you get older and kids finish college and get out on their own and the mortgage is paid off, you may no longer need to keep paying those monthly premiums.

There are two major types of life insurance policies: whole life and term insurance.

Whole-life policies combine life coverage with a potential buildup in cash value. There are many different kinds of whole life policies, and generally the premiums don't go up as you get older.

The other type of coverage is term insurance, which has no investment component. You buy life coverage that lasts for a set period of time, provided you pay the monthly premium.

For young people, premiums for term insurance are dirt cheap, so the earlier you buy one, the lower the premium and the better the potential payout. Premiums steadily increase with age, but by that time, perhaps your need for insurance has diminished.

I'm the first to admit that all types of insurance can be compared to gambling. If you don't have it, you are betting against all odds that you will never get sick, injured or die. Since the statistics show us that as we age, most of us get sick or injured, medical and long-term care insurance are pretty good bets.

It's guaranteed that all of us will die (at least I haven't yet heard of anyone who is immortal!), so, in my opinion, all types of insurance are gambles well worth taking, not only for your peace of mind, but for the health of your portfolio and your estate.

CHAPTER 5

Decisions as You Go Forward

Many people spend more time planning for a two-week vacation
than they spend planning for retirement.

—OLD SAYING

This chapter is about the many decisions you will need to make between now and the end of your life.

You're not near the end of your life, you say? Maybe. Maybe not. None of us really knows.

In any case, it is much simpler and less stressful to make these decisions, particularly end-of-life decisions, now when you are presumably healthy and mentally sound. It will be harder later, you can be sure of that.

Retirement: Yes or No?

Here's the first question to consider and the first decision to make: When do you retire? Or do you retire at all?

A recent Gallup poll shows we are retiring later and later and, interestingly, almost half of high earners—those whose incomes are $75,000 or more a year—don't plan on retiring until they are at least 70. Others who can arrange it cut back on hours, job share or start their own businesses. Full retirement isn't something that many Baby Boomers embrace these days.

Gone are the days when most workers were forced to retire at 65. Many of us are healthy long beyond that age. If you love your job or you love something about it, then why retire at all?

> *If you don't know where you're going,*
> *you might end up some place else.*
> —YOGI BERRA

Or, like one of my clients 20 years ago, maybe you just want the comfort level of knowing you can tell your boss to "take this job and shove it" any time you like. He was in his 50s and hated his job when he asked me to run all the numbers and let him know if he could retire. Once he got the assurance that yes, he could retire and sustain his lifestyle, he was ecstatic—and chose to stay on the job. Twenty years later, he's still there and even more secure in the knowledge that he can take walk away any day he likes!

As you move toward retirement, it's important to have plans. This may seem like a no-brainer to you, but trust me, over the years I've had a surprising number of clients who haven't really thought about what they'll do when they retire.

For some, retirement can be like getting off a 767 jetliner and suddenly finding yourself walking down a country road. It may seem wonderful and relaxing, but it could be exactly the opposite.

It's a time of re-imagining your life and moving into a new way of thinking, relating and be-ing in the world. The word "retirement" means to go away or withdraw. That's not what today's retirees want to do. A world of possibility is open to you.

I've had clients who were CEOs of Fortune 500 companies who had the hardest time in retirement of anyone. They were accustomed to having employees to do things for them and being in charge of everything. Then they retire and their wives are asking them to take out the trash. It's a big adjustment on both parts.

People who refuse to rest honorably on their laurels when
they reach retirement age seem very admirable to me.
—HELEN HAYES

I like to think of retirement as the time when you move from a successful career into significance. Retirement is a time, when, if you've planned well, you can make a significant difference in somebody else's life, on a charity or in your community. Maybe you'll volunteer at the soup kitchen or start up a non-profit to help abused women or finally pursue your passion for painting. Maybe you'll choose to have a second career or take a simple job. I have one client who decided to be a Wal-Mart greeter. Aware that most people would think he was taking the job because he was desperate for money, he stipulated that he'd be assigned to a store 30 miles from his little hometown so no one would recognize him. He's a social person and loves his new job.

It doesn't matter what you do in retirement, but it does matter that you *do something*. Remember, you could easily live 20 or 30 years more. Do you really want to spend it watching re-runs of *The Simpsons*? I didn't think so.

The time to think about your post-retirement life is *before* you retire. Few of us do.

This is a time when there are many other important and life-changing decisions to make.

Space and Place

Where will you live?

- Do you want to stay in your current home?

- Downsize?

- Move to a retirement community?

- Move to a sunnier climate?

- Move closer to your children or grandchildren?

- Move in with your kids?

There are many elements to each of these decisions. The decisions you make at age 60 or 62 may need to change as you get older and perhaps experience health challenges or your life changes through the death of a spouse or other factors.

I'm not here to tell you what are the right or wrong decisions, but to help you answer some simple questions and look down the road and make choices that will be lasting ones.

Let's look at them one at a time:

1. **Stay in your current home.** What will happen if you or your spouse become disabled? Is your entrance handicapped accessible or can it easily be made so? How about the interior—is your bedroom on the second floor? If you are thinking of a remodeling project, consider the aspects of aging in place including wider doorways to accommodate wheelchairs, zero clearance showers, grab bars and other modifications that will allow you to stay in your home as long as possible. Other considerations: Will a large home eventually become a maintenance burden? If you have a mortgage, will the mortgage payments be a burden if one partner should die?

2. **Downsize.** Will this mean relocating to a new neighborhood, a condo or even to a new city? How important is your neighborhood and your social support group there? What will you do when family visits—will there be space for them? Is that important? Can you afford to downsize? What is the cost of real estate at current prices versus the current value of real estate you may have owned for many years? Selling your current home is a big decision and it's a delicate dance to decide when the time is right to sell.

3. **Retirement community.** What will be the cost? What are the projections for cost increases over the next 20 or 30 years? Are you buying a unit or entering into a lease? If you're buying, what are the re-sale prospects? What will happen if you need assisted living or other skilled nursing care? Will you be required to pay for your apartment plus the skilled nursing facility? Ask yourself the same questions about change of location as in #2 above.

4. **Move to a sunnier climate.** The advantages of warm winters go without saying for many of us. Will you simply spend winters there? If so, who will

take care of your colder climate home? You'll need to factor in the extra costs and perhaps a mortgage on a vacation home property, which will not be tax deductible. Ask yourself the questions in #2 as well.

5. **Move closer to your children or grandchildren.** The questions of #s 2 and 3 apply here, too. In addition, consider your children's and grandchildren's lives. While it may be fun to attend your grandkids' soccer games and ballet recitals and share family dinners several times a week, will you really be invading their lives? Will you be welcome on a daily basis? What happens when the grandkids go off to college? When your kids retire and move to Florida?

6. **Move in with your kids.** Most of us would not choose this option, unless there are financial or health challenges that force it. There are exceptions that work very well, with grandparents sharing parenting responsibilities and household chores. The downside of this one is that, over time, children may feel burdened with the care of their parents and become resentful.

Space is an equally important element of where you will live in retirement. Independence is important to all of us. A sense of safety and security on your part and to reassure your children is important at this juncture. This is approaching the time when we need to have "The Talk" with our families. (More about that later in this chapter.)

Most of us want to take care of ourselves until we can't. Yet the multi-generational households of the past have become a growing trend today. I know a family of mother and child, grandparents and in-laws who share separate floors of one home quite happily. It might not be everyone's choice, but there are advantages to it on a financial, emotional and practical level.

Health care directives

Everyone should have a durable healthcare power of attorney. This allows a person you designate to make medical decisions on your behalf if you are incapacitated, whether by illness or injury. Many people designate their spouses as their health care agents, although this is not mandatory. You may not wish to do so if your spouse has health problems that might make this added responsibility extraordinarily difficult. This allows your agent to have access to all of your medical information, something that might not be possible without this legal document. You can designate as many alternates as you wish in case the person you have designated is not available. It's important that the person who holds your health care power of attorney lives close to you in order to advocate for you in the case of a sudden illness or accident. This may be one of your children (who is over the age of 18), a close friend or even an attorney.

Here are some recommendations from the American Bar Association to help you chose the right health care agent:

- Choose someone who will talk with you now about your wishes, who will understand what you want and your priorities about health care, and who will do as you ask faithfully when the time comes.

- Choose someone who lives near you or could travel to be with you, if needed.

- Choose someone you trust with your life.

- Choose someone who can handle conflicting opinions from family members, friends and medical personnel.

- Choose someone who can be a strong advocate for you if a doctor or institution is unresponsive.

You can find a universal health care power of attorney form at the American Bar Association's website: www.americanbar.org/content/dam/aba/uncategorized/2011/2011_aging_hcdec_univhcpaform.authcheckdam.pdf

This form is simple and self-explanatory. It must be signed by at least two witnesses. A handful of states do not accept the universal form. These are listed in the above link.

A living will, sometimes called a medical advance directive, is very similar to a healthcare power of attorney with the exception that it is limited to deathbed concerns only. It's used to specifically declare your wishes on life-prolonging measures if there is no hope of recovery. Living wills can include

"DNR," or Do Not Resuscitate orders if that is your wish. You can also include your personal wishes about transfusions, ventilators, kidney dialysis and other specific medical procedures in a living will.

Forms for living wills are usually available through your local hospital or doctors' offices, or at www.caringinfo.org

It is a good idea to have both documents and make sure they are readily accessible to your agents, as well as to your doctors and your hospital.

Durable powers of attorney

It's a good idea to prepare a simple power of attorney to allow your designated agent (a member of your family or not) to take care of your financial matters in the event you become temporarily or permanently unable to handle them yourself. Since these events can occur suddenly, it's a good idea to have them in place *before* you need them. This is a simple form that gives your agent (sometimes called attorney-in-fact, not to be confused with attorney-at-law) authority to conduct some or all financial transactions on your behalf. You may limit it to the payment of bills and personal obligations, or broaden it to allow your agent to buy and sell real estate and authorize investment transactions or anything in between.

This document is called a durable power of attorney because it continues until it is revoked or the signer dies. The written document must be witnessed. Sometimes banks and other institutions will require all of the signatures to be notarized.

Have a conversation with your banker and determine what is needed and how the bank will recognize your agent when the time comes. Then get those documents on file so the transition will be seamless.

A very rich person should leave his kids enough to do anything,
but not enough to do nothing.
—Warren Buffett

YOUR ESTATE

Wills

Everyone needs a will. Period. End of sentence. Unless you want the state to decide the distribution of your assets (which will have undoubtedly been gutted by legal fees) and the futures of any minor children, you must have a will.

Your will should specifically state how you want your financial assets, bank accounts, real estate and personal belongings distributed upon your death.

Do not assume that your spouse, if he or she survives you, will automatically inherit your entire estate. This is not always the case, and the absence of a will may unnecessarily complicate financial matters for your spouse in a time of grief. On the other hand, in most states you cannot disinherit your spouse, regardless of what your will says, provided you are not legally separated or divorced at the time of your death.

A will is a simple legal document. You can make a handwritten will and have it witnessed by at least two people who are not beneficiaries, but I strongly recommend that you get a lawyer to draw your will for you to minimize the risk of a challenge. Be sure to update your will as your wishes change or as your beneficiaries or your circumstances change.

I want to insert a couple of paragraphs about guardianships here. Most people of retirement age do not have minor children, but it surely is not impossible! Of course, you will draw up documents designating guardians for your minor children. Of course, you will have discussed this with your appointed guardians and they will have certified copies of the documents.

What is more likely for people of retirement age is that our children will want to appoint us as guardians for our grandchildren. I strongly urge you not to become the guardians for your grandchildren for this reason: If a child has lost his parents, he then suffers a double loss because he also loses his grandparents, who must assume the role of parents. This is a very different relationship. If there is any alternative, I urge you not to become parents to your grandchildren, for their sakes.

Trusts

Revocable or irrevocable living trusts are another matter entirely. These are somewhat complex documents that require a lawyer's hand, usually costing anywhere from $1,000 to $5,000. In some cases, a trust is not necessary if you play your cards right.

The intention of a trust is to minimize legal expenses and to avoid probate, a lengthy court procedure that can take months or even years to resolve.

Most trusts are structured so that a surviving spouse automatically inherits all of the property of the trust. Successor trustees are usually named, who take over upon the death or resignation (more about that in the 'For Your Kids' Eyes Only' section in the next chapter) of the surviving spouse. Successor trustees usually have broad powers to manage, liquidate and distribute the assets of the trust without court oversight. In some cases, successor trustees are insecure in their abilities to manage the trust assets. When they bring in lawyers to do those tasks, the costs can spiral out of control.

Property changes hands by will, deed or contract (a trust is really a contract).

Your financial advisor can help you in estate planning and assuring that all of your assets are properly titled so they can pass unencumbered as much as possible.

Charitable trusts

There are several types of charitable trusts. The main idea of these types of trusts is to allow you to support a charity you believe in while you are still alive. This is complex territory, and you definitely need the help and advice of your financial advisor to set it up and give you and the charity the maximum benefit.

A charitable remainder trust is the most common type. Let's say you give a million dollars to a charity and in return, the charity provides you with a set stream of income for as long as you or you and your spouse live. Upon the death of last donor (you or your spouse), the remainder of the funds given to the charity stay with the charity.

There are substantial tax advantages to this type of giving, depending on your tax bracket.

There is another type of charitable trust in which you give to a charity and the charity keeps the principal for a certain amount of time. After the agreed upon period of time, the principal reverts back to you.

I am particularly fond of Community Foundations because they can act as conduits. If a client wants to donate to ten different charities, the Community Foundation channels the funds appropriately.

You might ask, "Why should I give to charity? I want to give my assets to my kids."

My answer: Charitable giving continues as a living memorial. Your name is preserved for posterity. Knowing that their parents or grandparents contributed to building a new library or an endowment to a local college should give them pride.

Beneficiaries

Pay attention to the beneficiaries designation on your assets: investment accounts, IRAs, 401(k)s, annuities, life insurance policies, real estate deeds, etc. These can change as grandchildren are born, relatives die or other life changes occur. I advise my clients to review their beneficiaries shortly after the first of every year so they don't forget.

You can designate investment accounts, a savings or checking account as "transfer on death." This avoids probate.

I had a sad and fairly horrifying experience with one client, a university professor who was over the age of 70 when I met him. His estate contained more than $7 million. He was married with no children. The professor and I had a long conversation about estate planning, but, sadly, the professor's wife died a couple of months after we began working together. I e-mailed him my condolences and reminded him that he should change his will and update the beneficiaries. He replied that he had done so. I didn't find out until a year later, when the professor died, that he had updated his will to read literally that he left everything to "my three sisters," without specifically naming them. What a mess! Eventually, the courts awarded the entire amount (minus substantial legal fees) to the oldest sister. The other two sisters were excluded and the eldest sister was saddled with a huge inheritance tax bill. The eldest sister decided to share her inheritance with her two younger sisters, but there was nothing legally that required her to do so.

Having "The Talk" with Your Family

We definitely have taboos about money and death in our society. Most of us are really squeamish when it comes to talking about any of them and our levels of discomfort increase when it comes time to talk about these things with families and heirs.

Nevertheless, it's a talk you must have. If you don't, there may be arguments, misunderstandings and family discord if/when you become ill or incapacitated, widowed or after your death.

This may be one of the most important conversations you have with your family. If possible, gather the family together, although I recognize that with the far-flung nature of our families today that may not be possible. It's an emotional topic, because you'll be talking to them about health concerns and your death, so you might consider combining the celebration of a significant birthday or anniversary or retirement with the discussion of this subject.

If you have a trust, your trustees should have copies of the trust. If you have a will, the executor should have a copy of the will. I'm in favor of letting all the heirs know the terms of your estate, how it will be divided, charitable contributions you have made and more.

Yes, it might cause a little familial distress, but better while you're alive to handle it than after you're gone and your family disintegrates into squabbling or worse. As I write this, our little town in the mountains of North Carolina is transfixed by the local newspaper's excruciatingly detailed reporting of a civil lawsuit in which the children and other heirs are disputing the estate of a wealthy businessman.

If, for example, you have chosen to give different shares to each child, it's fair to explain why—or not. It's your choice. Let them know the basics of your estate, whether it is a will, a trust, a combination, and who is the executor/trustee. Let them know how you want your estate and your personal belongings to be handled, what they can expect to be in the estate and the legal arrangements you have made.

This is also the time to talk about all of those legal and medical contingencies. Put your financial powers of attorney and advance directives in place and give copies to those who hold them. Talk about long-term care, your wishes at the end of your life and your funeral planning. Be sure they have a copy of your long-term care policy.

Your legacy in personal terms

Aside from all the legalities around the issues that arise at the end of life, there are the more weighty issues of what you choose to leave behind. It's easy to pass on your money and your property. But that could be gone in a handful of years. The legacy of your family and its stories and history are more important. How many children today know the names of all of their grandparents? How many adults know the names of all of the siblings of their grandparents? What makes your family unique? This is your personal legacy and it is an important part of what you will leave behind.

Consider the following questions and discuss them with your family. You might be surprised how much your spouse and children will contribute to this conversation:

- What family history would you like future generations to remember?

- Are there specific traditions for family holidays or life events that you would like to be preserved?

- What favorite family stories should be documented?

- What values are important to you that you'd like to instill in future generations?

- What specific life lessons would you like to pass on to future generations?

- What contributions to society should be remembered?

- What household items or collections of emotional value would you like to see passed on to future generations?

- How should family photographs, journals, diaries and other important documents be distributed?

- How should valuable personal items (antiques, art, jewelry) be distributed? (Include a recent appraisal.)

The Talk doesn't have to be maudlin or morbid. In fact, you can inject The Talk with humor and family insider stories and jokes. Nevertheless, it's a good idea to put the basics in writing in a letter they'll all get a week or so later in case emotions color their recollections of what you've said.

Most of us think we have all the time in the world, but we may not. Grab the bull by the horns and take care of this while you can.

For your family: What they need to know

This is pretty simple and should be a no-brainer: Let your family know where to find all of the important documents they will need in the case of your serious illness, incapacity or death. Better yet, be sure your executor or successor trustee has a copy of everything pertinent. It's surprising how many people neglect this, sometimes with serious consequences.

If, for example, you want your body to be cremated, but your family doesn't have a document expressing your desires for the disposition of your body, it's likely you will have already been embalmed and buried before the documents are found. If you've pre-planned your funeral, be sure that your closest relatives have all of the information and documents for the same reasons.

And, please, please, please! Don't leave your will, trust documents and instructions to your heirs in your safe deposit box! Most banks freeze access to safe deposit boxes upon death and the delay in accessing these documents can create a nightmare for your executors or trustees.

Here's a simple checklist that your heirs should have. Please be sure to keep it up to date.

WHAT MY FAMILY NEEDS TO KNOW

Your name: _____

Date of birth:_____ Social Security #: _____

Your spouse's name:_____

Date of birth: _____ Social Security #: _____

CHILDREN*

Name	Date of Birth	Social Security #

* If any children are minors, who will have guardianship on your death and where are documents of guardianship?

GRANDCHILDREN

Name	Date of Birth	Social Security #

GREAT-GRANDCHILDREN

Name	Date of Birth	Social Security #

Where is your will? _____

Who has copies?_____

Who is executor of your will? _____

Name:_____

Address: _____

_____

Do you have a trust? ❑ YES ❑ NO

Who are the trustees?

Names: _____

Phone: _____

Do you have long-term care insurance? ❑ YES ❑ NO

Company information: _____

_____

Does your spouse have long-term care insurance? ❑ YES ❑ NO

Company information: _____

_____

Do you have life insurance? ❑ YES ❑ NO Amount:_____

Company information: _____

_____

Does your spouse have life insurance? ❑ YES ❑ NO Amount: _____

Company information: _____

_____

Do you have a property & casualty insurance agent? ❑ YES ❑ NO

Name:_____

Address: _____

Phone: _____

Do you have pre-paid funeral arrangements? ❑ YES ❑ NO

Where? _____

_____

Financial advisor

Name:_____

Address: _____

Phone: _____

Accountant

Name:_____

Address: _____

Phone: _____

Attorney

Name:_____

Address: _____

Phone: _____

Do you have a living will?   ❑ YES   ❑ NO

Where filed: _____

_____

Do you have a durable Power of Attorney (POA)?   ❑ YES   ❑ NO

Who holds durable POA?

Name:_____

Address: _____

Phone: _____

Do you have a healthcare POA?   ❑ YES   ❑ NO

Who holds healthcare POA?

Name:_____

Address: _____

Phone: _____

Do you have disabled children? ❏ YES ❏ NO

Do you have parents to care for? ❏ YES ❏ NO

Where are your bank accounts?

Bank: _____

Account#:_____

Bank: _____

Account#:_____

Bank: _____

Account#:_____

Bank: _____

Account#:_____

Do you have IRAs, 401(k)s? ❏ YES ❏ NO Amount:_____

IRAs, 401(k)s held at: _____

Pension: _____

From: _____

Include in your file:

❏ Birth certificates

❏ Marriage certificate

❏ Military discharge documents

❏ Life insurance policies

❏ Previous years' tax returns and supporting documents

❏ Personal notes to family, friends

❏ Your obituary

CHAPTER 6

For Your Kids' Eyes Only

OK, I know you're going to read this anyway. Please understand that this is written with the best of intentions. If you haven't already done so, I recommend that you give a copy of this book to your children.

There are delicate questions and milestones as we age. Sometimes we don't recognize the milestones, and it falls to our families to help us make the right choices.

Among them:

- How can you keep aging parents safe and comfortable in their own home?

- When is the right time to move them into a senior community or assisted living or nursing home care or into your home?

- How do you get Mom or Dad to surrender the car keys?

- How do you get a surviving parent (or both parents) to resign as a trustee of his/her own estate?

It is painful for children to see their parents age. Now the ball is in the family's court and difficult decisions have to be made, often against the wishes of aging parents who do not recognize the need for change.

Dealing with dementia

Alzheimer's disease and other forms of dementia have become more and more common. Half of all people over the age of 85 have some form of dementia, and it often manifests in mild forms for several years before that. If you notice that your parent has difficulty driving in once-familiar neighborhoods or has difficulty balancing the checkbook or forgets your birthday or gropes for words, you are quite likely dealing with some form of dementia. You can find a detailed list of symptoms of early cognitive impairment at the Alzheimer's Association website, www.alz.org.

If you are noticing any of these symptoms in a parent, seek medical advice. There are some drugs that may delay the progression of the disease. There are forms of dementia caused by nutrient deficiencies or chemical toxicity that can be reversed.

Among the many terrible aspects of Alzheimer's is that its victims typically do not recognize their impairment. They may become frightened and angry, combative and even violent. Personality changes may take place. This most likely will make it doubly difficult to persuade them to live in a more secure community or give up the car keys.

If your parent has dementia, it's going to be a tough road for everyone. You have my understanding and sympathy. I had siblings who suffered from the disease and some were in costly skilled nursing care for years, while others were cared for at home, both of which took a profound emotional and financial toll on the family.

If cognitive impairment is an issue when the difficult decisions need to be made, it may compound the difficulty.

Let's take a look at these questions one at a time and I'll offer some ways to address them. In the end, sometimes children have to become the parents and make decisions that may not make them very popular with Mom and Dad, at least for a while.

How to keep aging parents safe and comfortable in their own home

In most cases, Mom and Dad will want to remain in their own home. You can help out with cleaning and gardening chores or hiring helpers who can do that if you don't live nearby. It's important to be physically present as much as possible, although I am the first to recognize that widely scattered families cannot always do that. If cooking is becoming a chore, there is Meals on Wheels. If necessary, you may even be able to engage someone to help with bathing and other personal needs an hour or two a day.

If safety is a concern because the house has stairs or other hazards, you can get stair chairs or even consider moving the bedroom to the first floor so it is no longer necessary to climb the stairs. I am a big fan of those necklace-type alarm systems in case of a fall or medical emergency, but I realize that they may not always be worn.

I know an elderly woman who wanted to stay in her Midwestern home while all of her nearby family went to Florida for the winter. I suggested installing a nanny cam, a video surveillance system that the family can monitor by computer and know that she is moving around as would be expected. These cameras don't have to invade her privacy; they can be in the hallways, living areas and kitchen, but it has given her family members a great deal of peace of mind.

How to determine the right time to move your parents into a senior community or assisted living or into your home or from home to nursing home care

Sometimes fate intervenes and an illness or accident forces this move, but more frequently, the decision to leave a home becomes a mutual choice. If it's not a mutual choice, it becomes even more difficult when you have to tell Mom or Dad that is time to move. Perhaps they live far away from family members who can help care for them or they are in physical danger from falls. If dementia is an issue, safety considerations become even more important—for example, the ability to cook without starting a fire or water left running.

You may be able to help your parents make this choice when they realize that the upkeep on a home is more than they can or want to handle. If one of them has died, leaving the other one alone, the loneliness factor is a serious consideration. You may be able to convince Mom that she'll have fun playing bridge with the ladies in the senior community, or Dad that he can join gents his age at the gym and for coffee afterwards, or both of them that they'll find new purpose in life helping the grandkids with their homework and being embraced in the bosom of your family. Social support is a major factor in the continued health and well-being of the elderly and this can be an important part of your persuasion when the time is right for a move.

I'll recommend this throughout this process: Enlist the aid of the doctor. Most elderly people have great respect for doctors and they may be more willing to listen to advice coming from the doctor than from you. Respected family friends, their financial advisor or attorney may also be helpful in persuading them that it is time for changes to be made.

Surrendering the car keys

This is likely to be an early issue and an extremely contentious one. Just rest assured that if you feel you must force them into this decision, you are doing it for the safety of your parent and for the safety of others. Don't feel guilty.

The ability to drive equates with independence and no one wants to give up independence. Driving and domicile are often intimately linked: If Mom can't drive and the nearest grocery store is five miles away and no family members live close by, there may be little choice but to move her into a senior residence.

Sometimes, the elderly will make their own decision to stop driving when they realize their visual acuity is not what it once was or perhaps they chose to stop driving at night. Those with early- and mid-stage dementia may get lost on familiar routes. I have heard of cases where the police will intervene and give confused elderly people rides home, but if it happens more than a couple of times, most police departments will ask them to surrender their licenses. This can be very traumatic for these newly disenfranchised drivers, but it is done for their safety as well as for that of other motorists.

Doctors can and should help in the situation. In some states, doctors are required to confiscate driver's licenses of people they judge are not fit to drive. Make an appointment with your parents' doctor and have a conversation about this issue.

If the issue becomes very contentious, which it may, the last resort may be to your state's Department of Motor Vehicles. Most states allow anonymous complaints against drivers who shouldn't be on the road. In these cases, the driver is called in for a re-test. Failure to pass the vision test or the on-the-road driving test will result in the loss of the license. Check your state's Department of Motor Vehicles website to learn about the procedure.

I know of one person who removed the distributor wire on her father's car as he descended into severe dementia. She simply told him that the car wouldn't start (which was true). He forgot about it after a few days.

I don't recommend that you lie to your parents, but, especially if dementia is an issue, sometimes it is necessary to put off answers to some questions for their own safety or mental well-being.

Incompetence

Here is where we get into really murky waters.

Incompetence is a medical and legal term. Most estate planners include provisions for incompetence in wills and trusts. In most cases, a person may be declared incompetent to handle his/her own affairs with the certification from two doctors. Sometimes a person may designate a family representative or a family panel to make that decision.

A declaration of incompetence could be temporary, for example, when someone is recovering from surgery or an infection or some other illness. More likely, the declaration would be permanent, as in the case of those with Alzheimer's or other forms of dementia, when mental capacity will not improve.

Removal from the managing of assets is probably the most difficult issue or decision that a parent will make or you as a child may have to force. It is the complete surrender of independence, and it is very painful for everyone. It is also for the preservation of assets of your parents. I know of one case where an elderly woman in the early stages of dementia developed a late life gambling habit. She gambled away nearly half of her assets before her family was able to have her declared incompetent and preserve enough assets to sustain her for the rest of her life.

In the case of an illness from which recovery is possible, the temporary declaration of incompetence may not be as difficult as the permanent choice.

Your attorney or financial planner may be helpful in obtaining the signature on a document in which the parent acknowledges the inability to handle financial and personal affairs and resigns as trustee, if there is a trust.

In cases where reason and persuasion are unsuccessful, legal action may become necessary. This is never pleasant.

Finally . . .

Yes, I agree, some of these decisions are ones you'd rather avoid. But I'm a realist and I urge my readers and clients to be realists, too. Death is inevitable. Illness and incapacity are not inevitable, but they are likely. It's particularly emotionally challenging to discuss these things with your family.

I can only give you my best advice after seeing innumerable clients struggle with these issues and regret their inaction: Do it now, while you are healthy and strong. You and your family will be glad you did.

About the Author

Janet Metzinger has lived and breathed her work as a financial planner for most of her life, beginning with her "job" as a pre-school child to write down the commodities prices as they were read over the radio, assisting her father, an Indiana grain dealer.

She carried that early childhood work into her teens when she transferred prices from the ticker to the quote board in a broker's office.

After graduation from college, she dallied briefly as a teacher and basketball coach, but the world of finances called her again.

Since the early 1970s, Ms. Metzinger has owned her own financial services business. She incorporated in the 1990s as Executive Planners, Inc. in Indiana. In 2003, she moved her business to the small town of Brevard in Western North Carolina.

She has worked with clients all over the world, ranging from Fortune 500 CEOs and other high ranking executives to athletic directors and coaches at colleges and universities all over the country, with whom she has a special affinity after her brief career as a high school basketball coach.

"I never wanted to be the biggest, but I wanted to be the best," she says.

Ms. Metzinger has two daughters, five grandchildren and four great-grandchildren.

Her Executive Planners website is www.executiveplannersnc.com.

Ms. Metzinger is an Investment Advisor Representative with, and Securities and Investment Advisory Services are offered through Transamerica Financial Advisors, Inc. (TFA), member of FINRA, SIPC and a Registered Investment Advisor. TFA is not affiliated with Executive Planners. Non-securities products and services are not offered through TFA.